National Online Safety

This edition first published in 2017.

National Online Safety Educational Resources
www.nationalonlinesafety.com

In partnership with Online Safety World
www.onlinesafetyworld.com

ISBN 978-1-5272-1784-3

This wonderful little story has been created to help you understand what it takes to stay safe in the online world. It can be used as a story book at home or as a resource in the classroom. All you need is a hint of adventure to open up endless hours of wonder and excitement, while learning how to make safer decisions when using the internet.

Help Oscar make the right decisions so he can avoid dangers on his journey through the online world.

Oscar's Adventures in the Online World

JAMES SOUTHWORTH and SARAH GRAHAM

Oscar takes a trip to the online world,
On his tablet computer he flies, without saying a word.

Close to the screen, he holds on tight,
Exploring the Internet, no parents in sight.

Onwards and upwards, into the digital sky,
Swooshing between planets, flying way up high.

Playing music online is his first quest,
It's time to put his search engine to the test.

Classical Music

He soon finds a piano he would like to play,
But to play, the piano is demanding he pay.

Oscar now doesn't know what to do,
He's caught in two minds and really needs YOU!

What should Oscar do?

OR

A) Pay with Dad's Credit Card.

B) Tell the piano "no thanks" with strong disregard.

Oscar's Dad is angry as you've just spent all his money.

The piano you've just paid isn't even real,
He's just a nasty man whose hobby is to steal.

You picked 'B'? Great choice. Bravo!
On to the next adventure we go...

Onwards and upwards,
Into the digital sky.
Swooshing between planets,
Flying way up high.

Speaking to his friends is his next online mission,
Joining them on social media is his decision.

A message appears from a girl called Ellie-May,
He doesn't recognise the name but opens it anyway.

"Hi," says Ellie-May, "send me a funny photo of your face."

"Me?" questions the boy, as his pulse starts to race.

"Yes, I want to see it, you're really quite ace!"

Oscar now doesn't know what to do,
He's caught in two minds and really needs YOU!

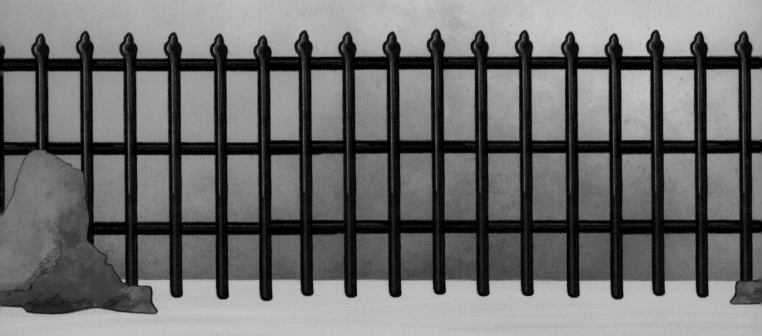

What should Oscar do?

A) Pucker up, take a snap and send the result.

OR

B) Ignore the message, block the sender and tell an adult.

You picked 'A'? Are you mad?
The outcome from this is really, REALLY bad.

Your funny face has been printed and posted in your school,
For Ellie-May is actually Jacob, your friend, the class fool!

You picked 'B'? Great choice, wahey!
Let's move on and be on our way...

Onwards and upwards,
Into the digital sky.
Swooshing between planets,
Flying way up high.

Online gaming is Oscar's next crusade,
A dragon game pops up that he has never played.

But why is he here? Oscar has no idea,
The big purple dragon just magically appeared.

Oscar now doesn't know what to do,
He's caught in two minds and really needs YOU!

What should Oscar do?

OR

A) Hold on tight,
click agree and then
start to play.

B) Close the window,
find a game he trusts
and be on his way.

You picked 'A'? Wow. Brave move!
You should not have done that, we all disapprove.
The dragon you want to play isn't a real entity,
He's a fire-breathing virus who has stolen your identity.

Onwards and upwards,
Into the digital sky.
Swooshing between planets,
Flying way up high.

Seeking a little alien is Oscar's final pursuit,
And it just so happens that Mars is en route!

He lands on Mars with no alien in sight,
Let's hope this last mission won't take all night.
Suddenly, out of nowhere, an alien appears,
He's a bit scruffy and fluffy, and has big long ears.

The adventurer snaps a selfie and posts it online,
Sharing photo evidence of the alien he finds.

Mean comments appear about his friend's unique style,
Making fun of the alien on Oscar's profile.

Oscar now doesn't know what to do,
He's caught in two minds and really needs YOU!

What should Oscar do?

A) Join in, have a laugh, and tell an alien joke.

OR

B) Don't join in, remove the pic, and report the mean folk.

You picked 'A'? Your decision is a disgrace,
The alien sees the photo with tears running down his face.
He wastes no time in reporting the crime to the police,
So get ready for your popularity to decrease.

You picked 'B'? Wahoo! You're right.
Let's fly back home at the speed of light...

The journey is done,
There's nowhere left to roam.
The boy has become tired,
And is now ready for home.

Oscar returns home feeling rather clever,
After making good choices online he feels safer than ever.

He turns off his tablet and closes his eyes,
He can sleep well, now he's internet-wise.

Oscar has prepared some activities for you!

I will never give out my personal information to anyone online. But what is my personal information?

Activity: Put a 'x' in the box if you believe you should not give out that type of information online.

My passwords ☐

The name of my school ☐

My phone number ☐

My date of birth ☐

My email address ☐

My home address ☐

My personal photos ☐

My current location ☐

A) All of the below are forms of personal information and should not be shared with anyone online.

To avoid people from hacking your accounts and accessing your personal information, you must have a secure password. To make sure it is secure, your password should be a minimum of 8 characters long and include at least one upper-case letter, one number and one symbol. Use the guide below to practice creating your own secure password!

1) Keyboard: Upper-case letters

A B C D E F G I J
K L M N O P Q
R S T U V W X
Y Z

2) Keyboard: Lower-case letters

a b c d e f g h i j
k l m n o p q r s t
u v w x y z

3) Keyboard: Numbers

1 2 3 4 5
6 7 8 9 0

4) Keyboard: Symbols

! " £ $ % ^ & * ()
_ - += {} [] : ; @ #
~ <> ?

Top tip: Never tell anyone your password, other than a trusted parent or guardian.

OSCAR'S TOP TIPS

for staying safe
in the online world.

ONLINE PAYMENTS

1. Always check with a parent or carer before buying anything online.

2. Get a parent or carer to read and accept the terms and conditions before making an online payment.

3. If an app or game asks you to pay for extras, always get permission from a parent or carer.

SPOTTING THE SCAMS

1. Never accept a friend request from somebody you don't know.

2. Never talk to anybody online that you don't know.

3. Be careful with sharing information online. NEVER give out your personal details to anyone.

4. Do not send or post photos online that you wouldn't want your family to see.

5. Be smart. You don't know who is on the other side of the screen.

RECOGNISING POP UPS & BAD LINKS

1. A web address beginning with httpS:// means the website is safe (the s stands for 'secure').

2. Never input your personal details into anything that you do not recognise or trust.

3. Check with a parent or carer before clicking onto a new website or app.

4. Get a parent or carer to install a pop-up blocker on your device.

CYBER BULLYING

1. Bullying is not OK, online or offline. Your actions could have serious consequences.

2. You can be reported to the police for using inappropriate behaviour online.

3. Feel confident to talk to a trusted adult if you see something that makes you feel uncomfortable online.

4. Be kind to others online and treat them how you would like to be treated.

CEOP

(Child Exploitation and Online Protection)

CEOP is a government agency that helps protect children from the dangers of the online world. If you see something online that makes you feel uncomfortable and you don't want to tell a parent or carer, you can report it to CEOP online!

To send a report to CEOP you need to:

1. Enter their website.
   www.ceop.police.uk
2. Click the link 'Make A Report'.
3. Next, click the boxes that apply to you.
   It will take you to a different page.
4. Click 'Start report' and fill out the form.

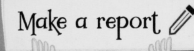

Alternatively, if you feel that you are being bullied online, you can call:

Childline (Under 18's): 0800 1111
NSPCC helpline: 0808 800 5000

You should always feel confident to talk to somebody about anything you experience online. It's NOT healthy to bottle up your feelings.

What is the name of your trusted adult?

My Online Safety Pledge

I will not give out my personal information online, to anybody.

I will not accept unknown friend requests.

I will not take part in any form of cyber bullying.

I will tell a responsible adult if I notice others being abused online.

I will not exchange photos & videos with anyone I have met online.

I will not meet up with anyone I have met online.

I will tell a responsible adult if I come across anything online that makes me feel uncomfortable.

I will not let my activity online disrupt my sleep, school work, chores, or relationships with others.

I will check with my parents before downloading or installing anything onto my device.

I will communicate with parents about new technology and help others understand internet safety.

I agree to follow the above rules.

Child signature: _____

Access to the NOS Parent's Online Safety Guide

At National Online Safety we make learning fun, interactive, challenging and memorable. We are proud to have developed learning materials that deliver key messages to children, parents, carers and teachers about how to stay safe online. We have developed a comprehensive, interactive, engaging Online Safety for Parents e-learning course that you can access via your child's school.

For information on how to access the parents' course please contact your child's school and ask them to contact us by email at hello@nationalonlinesafety.com or through our website (www.nationalonlinesafety.com)